7/12

WHO INVENTED TELEVISION?

PHILO FARNSWORTH

Mary Kay Carson

Enslow Elementary
an imprint of
Enslow Publishers, Inc.
40 Industrial Road
Box 398
Berkeley Heights, NJ 07922
USA
http://www.enslow.com

CONTENTS

WORDS TO KNOW

design—The way something is put together.

electronics—The parts and wires inside computers, radios, TVs, etc.

invent—To make something for the first time ever.

inventor—A person who creates something new.

plow—A farm tool that cuts and turns over soil.

Philo T. Farnsworth was only a teenager when he began to think about inventing.

WHO INVENTED TV?

Do you know who **invented** television? You might be surprised. One of TV's **inventors** was a kid. His name was Philo Farnsworth. He was only fourteen when he thought of a way to create TV pictures.

ON THE
MOVE

Farnsworth was born in a log cabin in Utah. His family moved to Idaho when he was eleven. Young Farnsworth drove a covered wagon to their new farm. A few years later the family moved again. This farm had something really new: electricity!

Farnsworth was born on August 19, 1906, in this log cabin.

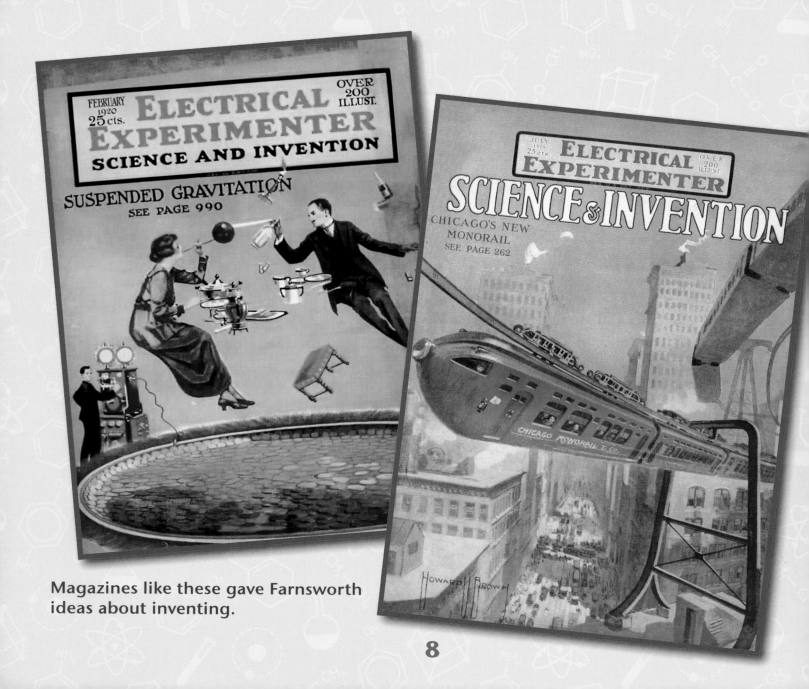

Magazines like these gave Farnsworth ideas about inventing.

FIX-IT
FARM
BOY

Farnsworth learned to fix the farm's electric machines. He read about **electronics** in magazines. He learned how wires and tubes made lights and radios. Farnsworth decided to be an inventor.

PICTURES MADE OF
LINES

Radio sends sound through the air.
What invention could send pictures?
Farnsworth got his idea for TV while watching
a **plow**. It cut row after row into the field.
The rows looked like lines on a page, or like
a picture sliced into tiny strips.

When Farnsworth was a boy, horses, not tractors, pulled plows and other farm equipment.

SOMEONE TO TELL

Farnsworth knew right away. He was right! Lines of light could send pictures from one place to another. But no one else understood his idea until he was in high school. Then Farnsworth told a teacher about it. Farnsworth even drew a TV camera.

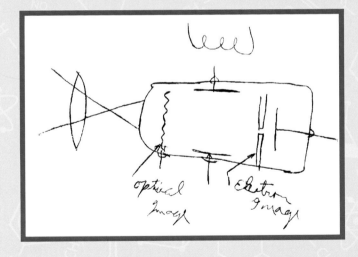

Farnsworth drew this sketch of a television camera for his high school science teacher.

SIGN OF
SUCCESS

Farnsworth kept working on his TV idea. When he was twenty, he built a TV system. It sent camera pictures to a TV in another room. One early TV picture he sent was a tiny dollar sign.

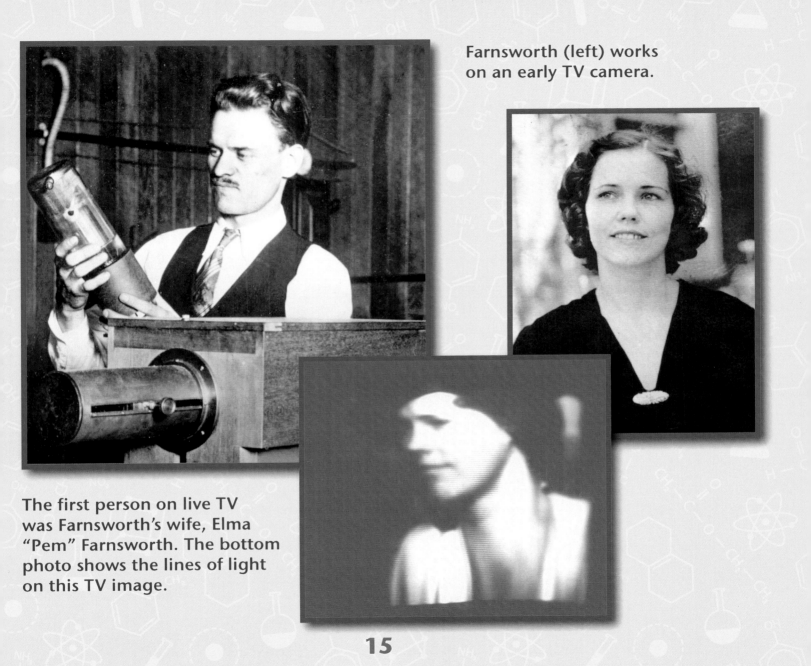

Farnsworth (left) works on an early TV camera.

The first person on live TV was Farnsworth's wife, Elma "Pem" Farnsworth. The bottom photo shows the lines of light on this TV image.

Philo Farnsworth's invention helped create the televisions we enjoy today.

MANY
PARTS

Other people worked on TV, too. In 1939 a company paid Farnsworth for his TV **design**. They added his invention to the work of others. By 1971, a TV had about 100 parts Farnsworth had invented.

Farnsworth turns a dial on an early TV.

OVER THE
MOON

This statue of Farnsworth is in Emancipation Hall in Washington, DC.

Soon many homes had a television. Farnsworth thought most shows were a waste of time. But he did watch the first moon walk on TV. Pictures were sent all the way from space! Farnsworth was proud to help make it happen.

Farnsworth lived until 1971. He was able
to watch astronauts walk on the moon.

ACTIVITY: CREATE A
CARTOON SHOW

You Will Need:

❖ lined index cards

❖ thick rubber band

❖ pens, pencils, or crayons

What To Do:

1. Stack at least six index cards, lined sides up.

2. Start with the top card. Draw a cartoon character toward the right-hand side of the card.

3. Go to the second card. Draw your basic character again in the same part of the card, keeping it the same size. (The lines will help with this.) Change something a little, like a smile, wink, wave, or kick.

4. Move on to the next card down. Draw the character again in the same place, but change something a little.

5. Keep drawing cards until you are happy with the changing picture. If the movement seems choppy, sandwich a new card in between two others and draw on it.

6. Wrap a rubber band around the left hand side of the stack.

7. Holding the stack with your left hand, use your right thumb to flip from top to bottom. Your cartoon moves!

LEARN MORE

BOOKS

Krull, Kathleen. *The Boy Who Invented TV*. New York: Knopf, 2009.

Niz, Ellen Sturm. *Philo Farnsworth and the Television*. Mankato, Minn.: Capstone Press, 2007.

WEB SITES

Physlink.com. *Who Is the Inventor of Television?*
<http://www.physlink.com/Education/AskExperts
/ae408.cfm>

The Philo T. Farnsworth Archives
<http://philotfarnsworth.com/>

INDEX

Enslow Elementary, an imprint of Enslow Publishers, Inc.

Enslow Elementary® is a registered trademark of Enslow Publishers, Inc.

Copyright © 2012 by Mary Kay Carson

All rights reserved.

No part of this book may be reproduced by any means without the written permission of the publisher.

Library of Congress Cataloging-in-Publication Data

Carson, Mary Kay.
  Who invented television?—Philo Farnsworth / Mary Kay Carson.
    p. cm. — (I like inventors!)
  Includes index.
  Summary: "Learn about Philo Farnsworth, and see how he invented tv"—Provided by publisher.
  ISBN 978-0-7660-3974-2
  1. Farnsworth, Philo Taylor, 1906–1971—Juvenile literature. 2. Electrical engineers—United States—Biography—Juvenile literature. 3. Inventors—United States—Biography—Juvenile literature. 4. Television—History—Juvenile literature. I. Title.
  TK6635.F3C37 2012
  621.3880092—dc23
  [B]
                                                    2011022629

Future editions:
Paperback ISBN 978-1-4644-0134-3
ePUB ISBN 978-1-4645-1041-0
PDF ISBN 978-1-4645-1041-7

Printed in the United States of America

012012 The HF Group, North Manchester, IN

10 9 8 7 6 5 4 3 2 1

To Our Readers: We have done our best to make sure all Internet Addresses in this book we active and appropriate when we went to press. However, the author and the publisher have n control over and assume no liability for the material available on those Internet sites or o other Web sites they may link to. Any comments or suggestions can be sent by e-mail comments@enslow.com or to the address on the back cover.

Series Consultant:
Duncan R. Jamieson, PhD
Professor of History
Ashland University
Ashland, OH

Series Literacy Consultant:
Allan A. De Fina, PhD
Dean, College of Education/Professor of
  Literacy Education
New Jersey City University
Past President of the New Jersey Reading Association

Photo Credits: © 2011 Photos.com, a division of Getty Images, pp. 3 (invent), 4; Architect the Capitol, p. 18; Couresy MagazineArt.org, p. 8, Farnsworth Archives, pp. 7, 13, 15, 1 iStockphoto.com: ©Antti-Pekka Lehtinen, p. 1, © Sean Locke, p. 2; NASA, p. 19; Nico DiMella, p. 20; Shutterstock.com, pp. 3 (design, electronics, inventor, plow), 12, 16, 21, 2 23; Utah State Historical Society, all rights reserved, p. 4 (inset, photograph has been colo enhanced); Wisconsin Historical Society, p. 11.

Cover Photo: © iStockphoto.com/Antti-Pekka Lehtinen (television); Utah State Historic Society, all rights reserved (inset, photograph has been color-enhanced).